Off The Short Leash

Diane Freed

Illustrations by Diane Freed

All People Press | Colorado Springs

Dedicated to my children and my Tribe.

"True Ignorance is not the absence of knowledge, but the refusal to acquire it."
Karl Popper

Contents

Whimsical

Unique Threads

The spider silk pants you did buy,
Got the deal you couldn't deny.
The flaws are minute,
On your new spider suit,
The only thing stuck is the fly.

The Pauper Speaks

Sat an old, lonely Pauper
In his shack, on a chair,
Who decided to break
From his quiet despair.

"Hey God are you there?"
Said his voice full of dread,
He heard a soft answer
In the walls of his head.

"Fear not and speak freely
I will answer your plea,
Your questions are valid
You can ask them to me."

The Pauper fell silent
To astonished to talk,
As the minutes ticked by
On the grandfather clock.

He asked God about time
When he started to speak,
"Is it measured the same
From a day to a week?"

"So, one million years"
Came God's soft reply,
"Is only a second

A mere blink of an eye."

"And what about money?
Gods have nothing to gain,
Spare change in their pockets
And a million's the same."

Said the still, quiet voice
"You're beginning to see,
A million's a penny
It means nothing to me."

The Pauper sat thinking
Of the best way to say,
His hunger was growing
With each passing day.

"Can you spare me a thousand?
Can you fill up my flask?
My needs are most dire
So I urgently ask."

Awaiting the answer
The room suddenly still,
Came the faintest reply,
"In a second I will."

The Master of Magic

Artist brushes bunched
Stiff hair standing at attention
Ready to be chosen.

White canvas calling an invocation
Magic begins
Thick brush liberating color.
Causing the white to vanish
Giving way to a colorful dance of swirls
An aura of a waltz
Leaving traces of a tango.

Warm pigment melting into cool
The craft of the mix
A fervent fluid flow.

Black bold lines
Conjuring contrast.
Small line brush
Hair tipped with ivory, dignified
Highlighting charms of wisdom
Twinkles of illumination.

Facial forms emerging
With wisps of hair flowing
An ethereal effect
Beauty of the spell is cast.

The Train Ride

Getting aboard the train with me
Requires a special pass,
Each ticket states 'I have respect'
To ride my cars of class.

No drama dumping is allowed
No self-absorbed complaining,
No rotten apples in the bunch
No pointed fingers blaming.

No lower minded shaming
Will enter any door,
No hidden self-agendas
These things we can't ignore.

I give my time and give a seat
To those whose hearts are true,
My educated tribe of love
Best trip we all pursue.

If you're riding Respect Express
Have your ticket for the route,
Leave all your baggage on the tracks
The train is pulling out.

The Illusion of Luck

I must be superstitious
The way I think and act,
When my clover has four leaves
And my mirror is intact.

I'm picking up that penny
Throwing salt behind my back,
I'll stay away from ladders
I'm not stepping on that crack.

Some point I'll see the folly
Change my thoughts to things concrete,
I really love black kitties
And my bunny needs her feet.

Are rituals all based in fear?
Lest my luck, somehow, is lost,
My knuckles sore from knocking
I'll just keep my fingers crossed.

Lucky Pick

When searching for a four leaf clover
I'd picked the entire patch,
Some different plants were in the bunch
Had to sort throughout the batch.

Many shiny leaves of Ivy
A misfortune to allow,
And I know what I'll be having
A rash of good luck now.

The Thrill of Getting Old

(Read to the tune of Michael Jackson's Thriller)

It's close to midnight
You shuffle to the bathroom yet again,
You rose too quickly
The shadows in the room begin to spin.

Face in the mirror
The horror looking back with bleary eyes,
Your heart is pounding
You realize you're paralyzed.

It's a thriller, chiller
An icy hand is sliding down your back,
Who's in the mirror?
Can't recall the creepy image staring back.

Where are your glasses?
You go to search the kitchen for a snack,
Under the moonlight
Rays coming from the door through every crack.

You shuffle forward
Your foot touches something solid on the floor,
It's soft and furry
It growls at you and scurries out the door.

It's a thriller, chiller
An icy hand is sliding down your back,
Pull on your sweater
That freezing wind is coming through the cracks.

The hounds are howling
Their hellish sound's enough to wake the dead
Secure your nappy
Then take your achy body back to bed.

It's a thriller, chiller
Time to get warm and comfy once again,
You took your sleep aid
So now this freakish night can finally end.

The Encounter

The first time I see you, you are walking at a good clip down the street, nearing the corner. After taking a look to the left, then to the right, you proceed across, the street deserted. Your breath briefly hangs in the crisp evening air, suspended momentarily, as an icy ghost before you, until you walk forward dispersing the vapors.

For me, it was 'love at first sight', the way you tugged down your winter cap so it hugged your ears, with your long jacket flowing in your wake.

I cautiously step forth from the shadows, making my way across the empty street, following in the indentions left by your snow boots. I continue along behind you for several blocks. Although visible in the street lamps yellow glow, I remain unnoticed.

A brisk gust of wind blows releasing some hair from your jacket collar as you shift the bag you carry from one arm to the other.

Walking up against a snow dusted row of bushes, I wonder if you will turn and see me.

Your pace begins slowing as you approach a tall building with an illuminated porch. In the soft light you plop your bag at your feet, your hands going in your pockets, searching.

I move up closer, now positioned directly behind you. I decide to make myself known, a timid "hello" escapes my mouth.

You turn around in surprise, your eyes wide. I feel a wave of compassion as you reach out and tenderly touch my face, then my head. "Meow", I whisper, "I love you too."

The Visit

There is a bird that visits me
    Lands on my windowsill,
        His voyeur eyes when looking in
            Can give me quite a chill

He often likes to bring me gifts
    He'll tap upon the glass,
        Showing off his shiny objects
            Found scattered in the grass.

He then tucks the gifted trinkets
    Between the wall and frame,
        Giving me a nictating wink
            He's off to fly again

I'm surprised as I discover
    When lifting up the sash,
        A plethora of pocket gems
            All hidden in his cache.

Most of the gifts are polished stones
    Or screws and roofing nails,

A tiny hinge from someone's box
Two shells from garden snails.

I've yet to find a golden watch
Or valued diamond blings,
Just buttons lost from winter coats
And bells with muted rings.

Once he brought a copper penny
And someone's silver key,
I'm grateful for the special gifts
He thinks to bring me.

The Jungle

All the cuckoo Ani birds
Who have gathered for a talk,
Assembled in Pochote trees
Above your yard they flock.

They proudly make their meeting known
All shared secrets they'll make clear,
Interrupting hammock time
Gifting droppings in your beer.

Don't plan on any quiet time
As they banter round and round,
You'll be tethered to your ear buds
'Til the meeting's slowing down.

Cicadas humming on the airwaves
Frogs begin to croak and jive,
With the Howler monkeys screaming
Know the jungle is alive.

FOREVER SAFE

The Goat Rescue

Goats' funny little antics
Reminds me of my clan,
Bouncy legs like baby Sis
Climbers like big brother Stan.

Each clever little personality
The beards swaying in the wind,
If you'd wear and not eat the hat
You'd resemble Uncle Ben.

With your chin's dangling dewlap
You could be my fat Aunt Pat,
Or my silly cousin Stewie
When you're burping loud like that.

I love working at the rescue
All the beards that I can comb,
Goat chorus with all the munching
I'm feeling right at home.

The Tea Party

As I walked by the garden
In the dim morning light,
Past the ficus and fringe
I saw a strange sight.

Sat a man at a table
A tall hat on his head,
"Won't you join us for tea?"
His raspy voice said.

"I don't see any 'us' here
I spoke looking around,
"Of course there's an us",
He said with a frown.

"Hare isn't here yet
Will be here in a while,
And my cat is right there
You can tell by her smile."

"Tea does sound quite lovely
I can stay for a bit,"
And with a tuck of my dress
I decided to sit.

"Pass it down to the next"
He announced pouring tea
I pushed the cup to my left

Though there only was me,
And the cat with the smile
Which was all I could see.

With a cup full before him
My cup got one drop,
"I believe we are out"
He said tipping the pot.

"Do you want crisps with your tea?
You may rather not,
They're a little bit soggy
It's been raining a lot.

"Now it's time for our meeting
We'll discuss here today,
How to punish pill pushers
And lock them away."

"Do these pills make you smaller?
Do some make you grow?"

"They end rabbit production
If you really must know."

"We'll take the pill pusher
And lop off his head,
And fill up our Kingdom
With rabbits instead."

Words dripping with sarcasm
He continued to say,
"If you're in a rabbit way
You'll just have to stay."

"You can't make me have rabbits!"
Was my shaky retort,
Pushing my chair back
The meeting cut short.

"When your Kingdom's overrun
No food left to share,
You're mad rules will result
In a world of despair."

"We will always have crisps
And probably our tea,"
Then he plucked poppy blooms
Beneath an Oak tree.

My transfixed eyes watched him eat
Each blossom he chewed,
Like the grin of his cat
He began to grin too.

"I'm done with your tea party
I'm done with your meeting,
I'm fleeing this madness
On the trail I'm retreating.

I searched for a fox hole
A small door in the Oak,
Found a large caterpillar
Through pipe rings of smoke.

The wise insect advised
"Keep your temper my dear,
Try one bite of my Trumpet
This mushroom right here.

The bite was quite bitter
But the shrinking began,
Now I slipped through the fox hole
To my garden again.

Yesterday's Tomorrow

Yesterday had shined so brightly
A fun brunch with someone dear,
Smiling faces all around me
Clinking glasses full of cheer.

Accomplished tasks without the rushing
Challenge met and handled well,
No clue of what Today would bring
No gut feelings did foretell.

But Today's not flowing smoothly
Minutes stepping out of time,
Forward path appears quite dimly
Void of glimmer, not sublime.

Hope Tomorrow keeps its distance
Staying off the heels of Now,
So brilliant rays of Yesterday
Can reach around somehow.

I can try to lift Today up
From the dark hole it resides,
So Tomorrow's chance is brighter
To be Yesterday's reprise.

Sugar and Sleep

Oh these brief winter days bring despair
Half awake eating pie in my chair,
This sugarplum treat,
Only thing that can keep
Me from crawling in bed with a bear.

Controversial

The Game

We are ancestors of the Indigenous,
Our land is taken,
Then you charge us rent,
Playing Monopoly with our lives,
No Free Parking,
Your Game board balancing,
On our bent, broken backs,
Our fingers spread in the dust,
Knees grounded,
As you race past "Go",
In your expensive Car,
In a High Hat and fancy Shoes,
Buying up the Avenues,
Weighing us down,
With your added houses and hotels,
Thimbles tucked away now,
Discarded Wheelbarrow,
Collecting dust down by the Railroad,
Meager provisions,
Distributed from the Community Chest,
Do we get another Chance card?
Stooping in our submissive positions,
Keeping the dice rolling,
But if we stand,
The Game is over.

Rants to a Politician

"Environmental Justice"
Chants the voice of the young,
And the 'woke' who have spoken
In their own native tongue.
Your policies are failing
Deceptions won't outfox,
We see your dirty fingers
Tucked in our ballot box.
Rearranging our laws
Just to make us feel heard,
While you're flushing the truth
Like an oil covered turd.
We are wise to the guise
Of your caring pretend,
As you lie through your teeth
With your shit-eating grin.
Your card tower of power
Will come tumbling down,
Since you used half the deck
Built with jokers and clowns.
Get up and take action
Put down your sweet tea,
Slavery is over
Let your captives go free.

The Plan

What to do with soulless monsters
With their evil, twisted plots,
Deluded leaders of bloodshed
They're taking drop by drop.

We'll redirect their mental ills
Pull the plug on all their cruel,
Coaxing them from ivory towers
New land for them to rule.

We'll promise them the Universe
We will take them for a ride,
Make their egos feel protected
Seated comfy, posh inside.

They'll know we handled everything
One-way tickets for the show,
The tanks are filled with rocket fuel
Off to Pluto they can go.

It's My Time

Am I the Baby's-breath to your Rose
arrangement?
Am I the off-white mat to your portrait?
Am I the throw pillow on your luxurious
sectional?
Maybe the footstool for tired feet,
Or the rug at your castle's entrance,
Keeping the mud out,
Making myself small to fit,
In the crevices of your large life.

I'm the hum behind your billboard megahit,
The stagehand as you steal the show,
An accomplice to your accomplishments,
Only the 'suc' to your success,
The broken rung in your ladder.

I'd rather be the Roses in the bouquet,
And the portrait on display,
Instead of the limp lettuce,
Under your culinary masterpiece,
I'm done with being the 'wo',
To your 'man',
The throw on your divan,
When will the time be 'myn'?

You say I can have a line,
In your next bestseller?

I will speak up,
And say'
If my name is included,
And only if I can have the last,
Word."

Don't Judge Me

I can tell by your bumper stickers
Your twisted screws are loose,
By your red-faced, angry phone chat
I can tell your tie's a noose.

I can tell from all the music
That's blaring from your ride,
You're deafening your sorrows
Behind window tints you hide.

I can tell by your fifteen kids
You're starting your own cult,
I can tell be your Facebook memes
Your life's lacking an adult.

I can tell by your boisterous voice
You want to be on stage,
I can tell be your incense smell
You're pretending you're a sage.

Bet you think I'm being judgy
With my calculated pitch,
And when a woman speaks her mind
She's often called a bitch.

Which is a judgment in itself
The conclusions we come to,
By assessing our surroundings
It's just what humans do.

The Walk

This jungle is dark
My feet hurt from walking
Heavy backpack
My arms going numb
My stomach growling
Louder now than my thoughts
I'm sorry to be complaining
I'm happy you are with me big brother
I do miss Mom.
She says it's safer that we left
Away from the man who tried to hurt us
Where are we going again big brother?
Land of Freedom you say
Not Land of Privilege
That's confusing
What is Privilege?
Where only some have Freedom you say
We want to be able to go to school
Be free to study what we want
Be who we were born to be
Be safe
From harm and persecution
I forgot what that means
That's where
Bad men can take us
Leaving our faces pressed against cold bars
Looking out like a zoo animal
Trying to see if Freedom is in the distance

We need to go
Where our arms and faces are the right color
Where it's safe to be a girl
With no slave labor
Maybe we can have a meal
I hope we get there soon
I'm hungry
I want to be safe and eat
I can't wait to hear those Freedom bells ringing
Instead of my grumbling stomach.

How to Write a Banned Book

When writing a book to get banned,
Same-sex love is sure to get slammed
And history of slaves,
How white men behaved
This knowledge will likely be damned.

And make your protagonist be,
A part of the LGBT
F-bombs you can shout,
Details don't leave out
So the self-righteous can disagree.

Colors of Love

Thank you loving person,
Who read to my child today,
Your kind voice,
During library story hour,
Confidently wearing your vivid colors,
Expressing your accurate version of You,
Being true to yourself,
An example for others to be true too,
Shame has no place here,
Pure joy is clear,
Happy children,
A safe place for smiles,
Colors of Love.

Relationship Dynamics

When you're adding one to a couple,
Your partnership needs to be supple.
Jealousies left behind,
As your love is combined,
Considering now you're a throuple.

Just Saying

Don't bite the hand that feeds you
It's the hand that lifts you up,
Together we'll find common ground
Drink from the common cup.

We two provide the company
Agreement gives us power,
We're striking when the fire's hot
Spark in our darkest hour.

The penny I've been saving
Is the penny we have earned,
The time is now to come old dog
Show me all the tricks you've learned.

There's no time like the present
I've dropped the penny in your well,
Led my horse to drink your water
Chosen heaven over hell.

So, show me all your magic ways
To entice my horse to drink,
We are better late than never
My pen's mighty with your ink.

The Sacrifice

Your babies are tossed when they're born,
Mama Cow your eyes look forlorn.
With your puss-laden breasts,
Back to pumps to express,
While the industry leaves you to morn.

The sacrifice doesn't end there,
So, women you need to beware.
When consuming the lot,
All the hormones you bought,
Cancer asks for a breast you can spare.

*As the medical establishment has gone back and forth on the dairy consumption and cancer link of reproductive organs, a recent study conducted in March, 2023, shows the link. The study follows 52,795 women for 8 years and found a high intake of cow's milk were associated with a 50% increase for breast cancer.
(www.pcrm.org/news/news-release/dairy-consumption-linked-prostate-ovarian-breast-cancer-finds)*

What We Can Not See

A chainsaw in the Amazon,
Like a cancer stick,
Chipping away at our planet's lungs.
Black soot falling from forest fires,
Embedded in our Polar ice,
Warming, melting.

The great Pacific Garbage Patch,
Plastic bags and bottle caps,
A circling whirlpool,
A current issue.
Abandoned nets and traps,
Lining the ocean floor,
'Ghost fishing',
Catching the unsuspecting.

Walls hiding animal ag,
No windows with glass,
No one wants to see,
Depressed workers getting PTSD.
What to do with cesspools?
Red and brown spray,
Raining down on people,
Smells like money.

Family day at the beach,
Running in the waves,
Resting in the sun,
Under the thinning ozone,
Comfortably numb,
Hidden 'dead zone' out past the waves,
Miles wide.

Time for the picnic lunch,
Consuming, tossing.
Contributions to the problem,
Habits without solutions.
What if we opened our eyes,
Wider?
Could we see,
That which is hidden,
In plain sight?

Mistaken

We look different than our Shepherd
But our hearts are quite the same,
We love our babies and our families
Experience fear, loss and pain.

With dogs nipping at our heals
And protecting us at night,
Whose yellow eyes are in the forest?
We'll be safer when it's light.

Feeling free from outside harm
Is it kindness done with care?
This ruse is quite misleading
Selfish reasons can compare.

We see his knife blade coming
Is the wolf the one we fear,
In the end it is the Shepherd
Who's intentions now made clear.

Soulful

Angel Advocates

To all the animal advocates
I raise my glass to you,
Helping those receive their justice
Change that chauvinistic view.

Standing strong in your convictions
Thanks for everything you give,
Keeping foxes out of fashion
Giving wolves a chance to live.

Ending animal experiments
Legal action changes laws,
No importing of big trophy heads
No smuggling macaws.

You're standing by the transport truck
To give a pig a drink,
Your 'adopt don't shop' protest sign
Might make a person think.

Those jailed in their confinements
No knowledge of a crime,
You are working hard to free them
Within constraints of time.

A better life beyond those bars
A place where freedom knows,
No dancing bears or elephants
Nonexistent captive shows.

Antidepressants for the orcas
They'd make a different choice,
These sentient ones who need our help
For the voiceless, you're their voice.

A Letter to My Children

Our once thriving, vibrant home
The Earth we call so blue,
Is slowly changing colors
Slaughter red is its new hue.

I'm sorry my sweet children
Wish I had good news to share,
No rescue will be coming
Those in power couldn't care.

You'll inherit all our mess
It's embarrassing to say,
We wrapped it up in plastic
Just to throw it all away.

I'm not sure how much water
Will be left for you to drink,
We used it for the fires
Need to filter it, I think.

And speaking of our water
Our cows need a drink, you see,
A million rows of feed corn
Where those forest used to be.

Our climate's a hot topic
Hard to watch our planet burn,
Our wild in silent exit
As it leaves with no return.

I'm sorry about the bees
Toxic cides were just too much,
We left a giant footprint
Trashing everything we touched.

I wish we had been better
Keeping greed off planet blue
If I had a time machine
I would change a thing or two.

Growing Hope

A single seedling surfaces
An unlikely growing place,
Emerging through a concrete crack
In search of sun's embrace.

The smoke is clearing in the dawn
With the ceasing sound of strife,
Among such saddened tragedy
A ruderal hope of life.

A sunflower of resilience
Sprouting peace in warring zone,
Who's finger let the seed slip through?
Hope they made it safely home.

For the people of Ukraine.

For Now

This wasn't my plan,
Sleeping in my Bru(Subaru),
Foam cushion in the back.
Parked behind the gas station,
Under the trees,
Owner knows I'm there,
For now.

My car, an act of optimism,
Someday I'll have gas money,
Priorities,
Food, water and a working phone,
Ready for that interview call.
Job hunting on foot,
Lots of walking,
Mildly warm days,
I'm lucky,
For now.

Miss my newspaper printing job,
Power of the digital age.
That last rent hike,
Final straw,
Savings gone.
Washing dishes for cash at the restaurant,
Raking leaves,
For now.

Appreciate the soup kitchen meals,
Especially the cruelty-free ones,
Provided by Food Not Bombs,
Sidewalk service,
A meal with a smile,
Kind greetings,
Provisions without proselytizing,
Long line for hot cocoa,
Hands reaching for a cup,
Missing fingers,
Frostbite.

Street life is sad,
Some sleeping on park benches,
In ditches,
On sidewalks,
Stone for a pillow.
Young person walking slowly,
A skeleton with skin,
Baggy pants cinched up,
Good use of a jump rope,
I offer my jacket,
A look of bewilderment,
"I have another," I reassure.

Not all my friends know,
A few offer a shower,
Some, a sofa to sleep,
I'm not wanting to camp,
In the center of their lives.
Not good for a woman to be on the streets,
But I tell them,
It's just for now.

Simple Life

Let's go inside the woods to live
Where the peacefulness resides,
This simple life with absent strife
Its healing balm provides.

Our warrior wounds can freely rest
World's pressures we'll dismiss,
We'll pass on second servings
Of life's circumstantial dish.

Has our mission been replaced
We brought to earth to share?
Need to relocate empowerment
To redirect, repair.

We'll rub away those calluses
Of unrelenting toil,
Time to tap our gifted talents
Plant those special seeds in soil.

As we nurture one another
We watch our talents grow,
Within rejuvenation
Our gifts begin to flow.

Surrounded by our tribe of wise
Souls attached with common thread,
We will disregard the rat race
Choose a simple life instead.

Best Gift

What is the best gift to give?
To a stranger,
It may be a smile.
To a homeless person,
It may be a meal,
Or a warm drink.
To a mother with youngsters,
It may be a helping hand with groceries.
To a neighbor,
A gift of time to help with a project.
To an elder,
A position in front of you in a long line,
An open door,
A glimmer of purpose.
To a child,
A gift of full attention,
Eye contact,
Gentle explaining,
An uplifting story.

To a troubled friend,
A gift of listening,
A kind word,
A warm hug with measurable intensity.
Each of these gifts ,
Are also for you,
And the nicest gift of all,
Is the chance to be your very best.

The Run

Crisp, damp morning air
Filling my lungs on the inhale,
Cool evidence with the exhale,
Arms extended,
Muscles reaching their furthest point,
Stretching,
Shaking out my hands,
My legs,
Sun on my back,
Ready to run,
Slow decent down the hill,
No pressure of a race,
Only my tranquil mind.

On level ground,
I increase my stride,
Gravel crunching,
Beneath my feet,
A rhythmic beat,
Breath deepens.
Plant life on either side of the trail,
Succumbing to a soft blur,
A Blue Jay alerting my approach.

Trail opens to a bend,
Creek running along side of me,
Challenging me to keep up,
Setting my pace,

Exhilarating endorphins,
Coursing through my body,
A vow to run until the flow is silent,
When creek meets pond,
Water twirling a calm mix.

Turning, I start my ascent,
More deep breaths,
Feeling the sun's warmth,
Basking in the rays,
I close my eyes.

When I open them,
I see my hand gripping my wheelchair break,
Then both my hands reach back for the cold
wheels,
I spin my chair toward the parking lot,
Car parked up front,
Ramp down, ready,
I love my morning runs,
In my tranquil mind.

Missing Mother

My Mother, my pearl,
My eyes miss looking into yours,
Connecting to your soul.
My ears miss hearing your voice,
Hearing your laughter,
Listening to your wisdom.
My arms miss enveloping you,
Into a warm embrace.
My voice misses sharing with you,
The secrets of my thoughts.

Sometimes I speak out loud,
While placing flowers in a vase,
"I love you bunches," I say,
My voice reminds me of yours,
Same pitch and nuances.

My hands in the soil,
Reminding me how much you loved to garden,
These could be your hands,
Brown sun-kissed spots,
Protruding knuckles,
Wrinkles in the right places.

I walk the same garden paths you once did,
Sometimes I glimpse your reflection in the pond,
Softening the sharp edges of missing you,
I feel your close proximity,
Your energy around me,
Soothing my soul,
My mother, my pearl.

My Firstborn

My precious, tiny firstborn,
A thread from fibers of my being,
Connecting us.
I was your oxygen,
Your subsistence,
Your protector.
I created you my 'child',
You created me a 'mother'.
You gave me new vision,
An awakening to see beyond myself,
You expanded my world,
You expanded my heart.

Being Teen

Elder propped against the door jam,
Like a soon forgotten broom,
You're sporting headphones with a mic,
Chosen remedy for the verbal constipation.
Delving into a pixel fantasy,
Claiming control over the controller,
Adrenaline addiction,
Taken to the next level,
Thumbs awaiting workout,
A low-injury sport.

Still tethered to your adolescence,
Stretching cautiously,
For the ledge of the Adult,
Uncertain where your grip will land.

Adopting idols fit to follow,
Selecting screen saviours.
Thorough searching the whole puzzle,
Looking for welcoming space,
Where your jagged piece can fit,
Careful not to over sand your edges,
For the purpose of conformity.
Classmates,
Navigating their altered states of escape,
Others checking out for good.

Dripping in style,
Walking the kaleidoscope halls,
In a hormonal haze,
Looking for the survival guide,
To this emotional galaxy,
Tips for traversing uncharted territory,
Finding that exceptional life raft,
A special someone to attach yourself,
Who reunites you with your secrets,
Floating confidently,
In troubled waters,
Identity crisis averted.

In maneuvering these teen years,
Apply a small amount of fortitude,
And a generous heaping of perception.
Fill your head with useful knowledge,
And your heart with coping skills,
Come away with visual clarity,
For an optimistic path,
Headed down the road,
That we call Success.

Wise Old Tree

What advice can you give me Old Tree?
Can you whisper your wisdom to me?
With your quiver of leaves,
In the mid-summer breeze,
Heard: Slow breathing my exhale is key.

Old Tree

Hello old Tree that grows in our yard. I see your branches outstretched embracing the day. Are you trying to touch the sun? I can feel your presence as I work in the garden below. You, the silent witness, standing, centrally located in our yard and in our lives.

The old constructed wooden bench you wear as a skirt now has a tighter fit. I guess an upgrade is due.

How many changes have you seen in our lives played out beneath you? You were there as our baby girl took her first courageous steps forward, making her way across the grass.

You provided your perfectly sturdy branch to attach her swing. Her small voice filling the air with her invented melodies, swinging and singing.

Our neighborhood games of kickball. You and bench were always home base.

You held many nests of little lives secretly hidden under your protective canopy. Precious additions, and some losses. Remembering the time we had to say goodbye to our beloved kitty. We placed her carefully in a box and laid her in the earth cradled between your roots. The ground sprinkled with tears of love.

Several leaf angels indented in your autumn carpet, laid golden at your feet. A couple months later, the snow angels made below your winter boughs.

Our daughter's first kiss in the shadows on a moonlit night. What secrets do you keep Old Tree?

The following summer you watched as the yard came alive again with the joyous voices of laughter, our daughter's graduation party.

We appreciate you being with us Old Tree. Someday soon our new grandbaby will take her first steps and play under your watchful eye. As for now, our garden has given its last yield of the season.

We make our way to your bench, which is new and larger to accommodate your growth. The two of us sit back to soak up a ray of afternoon sunshine, resting against your strong trunk. A gentle breath of a breeze loosens several leaves. They gracefully glide down, landing on our weathered hands and faces. We smile. Autumn is just around the corner.

A Much Needed Drink

Oh beautiful bird
On wings lifted high,
Pushed out from the heat
Of the hot, orange sky.

Smoke signals the danger
To chaos below,
Of fast-paced destruction
With the forest aglow.

The wild in their panic
Fleeing flames angry tongue,
Dodging droppings of embers,
Rushed, leading their young.

Trees anchored in place
Awaiting the blaze,
A roar taking their last breath
And a snap in the rage.

Humans race to save structures
Wet ash falling wistfully,
Historical mementos
Now becomes history.

Clouds usher in promise
Thunder voicing concern,
Columbines sway a rain dance
River thwarting the burn.

From a sprinkle to pour
The sky begins weeping,
The river runs black
From the soot that was seeping.

Strong winds part the clouds
Setting sun's last goodbye,
The beautiful bird
Now a speck in the sky.

The Beach

Oh, beautiful beach,
Meeting the incoming waves of turquoise,
Tumbling your tiny grains of wet and drying
sands,
Is your sand measuring time?
Or is the place where time stands still?
Freed from its hourglass.

Footprints indicating where we've been,
Until cleansing waters wash them away,
A path no longer traceable,
A past no longer necessary.

Waves hugging our weary bodies,
Worries of tomorrow sail away,
A bubbly foam of celebration
Champagne, crashing against your warm sand,
In and out,
Like the flow of breath,
Reminding us,
All we have is now.

About Leaving

When my body is done,
And I am gone,
Sprinkle me in the depth of the forest,
Just off the hiking trail,
So I can run with the Whitetail,
And sleep with the Red Fox,
I will cling to the dust of the earth,
So when you come for a visit,
I can walk the mountain with you.

Lifted up on talons strong,
I will perch on a tree branch high,
I will chant in the voice of the song birds,
And echo's soft reply,
Reminding you how much you're loved,
Each time you hear a Warbler's trill.

I will join the steady flowing spring nearby,
To float in her gentle currents,
Resounding my passions in her turbulence,
Voicing, "You are loved."
I will be your apricity,
Enveloping you in a comforting hug,
Always with you,
Always near,
My heaven resides with you,
Even on dim days.

When you embrace your mother tightly,
Hug her extra long,
I am there,
Suspended in time,
Holding you too,
Reminding you how much you are loved.

In the wee morning hours,
Before the light pushes the night aside,
Listen carefully,
I will whisper gently in your dreams,
"You are loved."

Autumn Magic

Grasshoppers arcing across the landscape.

Rows of grapes on the vine, ready for the wine.

Pumpkins line the fence, grinning faces on display. Accompanying a congregation of American Crows carrying on their cacophonous cackle about the weather, eyeing the letter formation of their southern-bound migratory friends, moving echelons across the sky.

Strolling through the bustling Farmer's Market, evident of the successful growing season. Apple boxes bountifully stacked, a multitude of gorgeous varieties; Pink Ladies, Gravensteins, Yorkshire, Northern Spy, Empire, Goldrush and Snapdragons.

Leaves rustling in anticipation of release. Golden yellow leaves flagging us to slow down. Crimson reds reminding us to stop from our hectic harvest pace. Trees taking in the sun's warmth, sending forth their long shadows across the earth.

Watching the ravenous wasps dive-bomb our dinner plates, desperately drinking the droplets of our sweet liquid from the bottom of out abandoned cups.

Soon the cool air begins to settle in the valley. Daylight waning in silent departure. Time to pull on our sweaters and gather wood for the bon fire.

Creating a cozy circle with our chairs, gravitating toward the fire's glow. The radiant Harvest Moon elevated above the silhouetted pines, casting her shadows like a spell.

We gingerly sip our mugs of hot apple cider, while reflecting on each other's shared stories of the past year, with thoughts of appreciation. Our voices rising in waves of laughter and song, with the pull of the moon. A small, sacred circle of friends who have come together to embrace this magical autumn evening of gratitude.

Ending the Plight of the Bumble

Your request to buzz the flower
Always granted any time,
Stay and linger for awhile
Know your presence is sublime.

Each blossom with its landing pad
Glowing ultraviolet muse,
My bee garden's cleared for safety
As no toxins have been used.

With your optimistic yellow
And your body cute with fuzz,
Landing light on nimble struts
Greeting every bud you buzz.

As you carry your Ambrosia
Valued cargo stored on board,
Gearing up for distribution
Gratitude for life's reward.

When your summer travels finish
Gardens all becoming bare,
Be selective of your hanger
Choose your winter home with care.

The leaves of my deciduous
Until spring, will stay in place,
No loud blower will take your roof
In sleep's silent, soft embrace.

Playful

A Birthday Poem for Dylan

I held your smallness in my arms
Wrapped in your blanket tight,
Your precious face was peering out
Eyes squinting at the light.

Born magnificent and perfect
You've grown with every year,
I'm blessed with all our memories
My cherished grandson dear.

Golfing with your plastic clubs
Tall castles built with blocks,
Found dinosaurs among my plants
Our hiking and long walks.

All these moments we have shared
Made arts and crafts to keep,
Danced to the band in Bancroft Park
Read books to fall asleep.

At seventeen you're now a man
Transforming from a boy,
Your strong, kind heart makes me so proud
You fill my world with joy.

For my beloved Dylan. Happy Birthday!

Drum Circle

You came to the drum circle,
With your tiny tambourine,
Bouncing off your swaying hip
Symbols' jingling joyous ring.

You listen closely for the beat
The maracas have begun,
The shakers add the harmonies
Elders' hands upon their drums.

A communal celebration
You enjoy the joining in,
To add your contribution
To the circle's vibe within.

The Candy Shop

We're skipping to the candy shop
With your tiny hand in mine,
Decision on the one to buy
Time for spending your last dime.

Sweet aromas swirl around us
Many choices vast and wide,
Pretty, brightly colored wrappers
Delights waiting to be tried.

You're smelling all the licorice
Strongly focused on your prize,
You're passing up the sours and mints
And no Gummies, I'm surprised.

You announce that you are ready
Hold the dime out for the buy,
To place the order of your choice
A big candy you will try.

You say you know the perfect one
But you're looking for a mix,
A caramel-truffle-toffee-fudge
Jelly-cherry-cordial-Twix.

(say that one fast)

Wind Dancing

You promenade the gathered clouds
You stir up quite a show,
Leaves leaping in a spinning swing
A dizzy do si do.

Your rumba gusts cause birds to hide
Light poles to tilt and sway,
Birch branches bend in steady gales
Bow in a forced plie'.

You can put away your jazz hands
Stage right you can sashay,
We're done with all your blustered calls
And dancing for the day.

At the Cabin

Sitting on the portico
　Greeting dawn's incoming gleam,
　　In my red Adirondack chair
　　　Warm snow rises into steam

Chirpy song birds waking up,
　Torpor leaving for the day,
　　Refreshing air enticing flight
　　　Calling critters out to play.

Hands warming from my coffee cup
　Hearing "Chickadee-de-des",
　　Nuthatches playing tic-tac-toe
　　　Up and down Aspen trees.

Melting ice releasing pine boughs
　An acoustic drip, drop, drip,
　　Surrounded by the sounds of life
　　　In my chair I sit and sip.

Chipmunks flipping leaves and searching
   For hidden future stash,
      Black squirrels relay from tree to tree
         Seven yard's the practiced dash.

Crows calling to their lifelong mates
   Fading echo's last reply,
      Their calculated nesting sights
         Which branch is best to try?

Soon Bear will wake from winter's sleep
   Join spring's chorus of the thaw,
      I'll sit and sip with drips and flips, and
         Crunching leaves beneath his paw.

Bear Necessities

Oh little bear tucked near Mom's side
Scents of summer wafting in,
Your curious, wondering mind
Brings you bravely from your den.

There's lurking dangers to beware
Mom will teach you these in time,
With rushing streams to play with fish
And sturdy pines to climb.

Taste testing your surroundings
Where campers left their trash,
Exploring rotting logs and leaves
Watching hoppers in the grass.

Eating honey, nuts and berries
A delightful recipe,
Then a quiet spot for napping
Is a bear necessity.

Dog Walking

Dog walking, a fun side hustle
Little's needed for the gig,
Exercise while making cash
And the nature payoff's big.

If jumping rope is not your thing
A shorter leash is best,
Bring a thick and sturdy one
You can disregard the rest.

Now's the time to enjoy your job
With sunshine and fresh air,
Good walking shoes upon your feet
Gentle breezes in your hair.

When walking off the beaten path
With a big breed by your side,
A crazed attack is very slim
Try to set your fears aside.

That poo bag dangling from your hand
Good substitute for mace,
A weapon of mass excretion
Adds surprise to someone's face.

If dog walking is your calling
Grab those leashes and that bag,
Because many pups await you
Go and make their tails wag.

The Rhythm of the Walk

Your gait is fluid music
Your tail swinging to a beat,
Your feet drumming on the pavement
Singing 'hi' to those you meet.

Your syncopated rhythms
Of your prancing and your sway,
Vibing on those compliments
Acquired along the way.

Moving out in front of me
As you smile from ear to ear,
Walking is your favorite sport
Your preference made quite clear.

Investigating odorants
To uncover what lurks deep,
Back and forth across the trail
Completes a thorough sweep.

You may not be quite ready
To the house we must embark,
It's time for a siesta
Dreams of walking in the park.

Little Tornado

You're my pudgy, playful puppy
Legs move the speed of light,
Your zoomies spin me like a top
No slowing down in sight.

Like a natural disaster
Came blowing through the door,
Abandoned massacred stuffies
Parts scattered on the floor.

Eventually you'll stop to stare
A stuffy I bequeath,
You'll jump on me and bite on me
With tiny t-rex teeth.

Established boundaries is the key
I'm sure it will take time,
The squeaky toy belongs to you
The fingers all are mine.

Doggie Yoga

Doggie Down Yoga Class was full
With intentions set on play,
It took a stretch to settle down
For the practice of the day.

Chanting 'howl's our mindful mantra
We sit to salute the sun,
Our drishti is the dog treat can
We'll be manifesting some.

We're good to do most any pose
But the one that's like the Cat,
At times it's quite the Slip-n-Slide
For those drooling on their mat.

Extended Puppy pose is rad
"Let's do Tree pose," we all beg,
Must remember to check our aim
With the lifting of our leg.

Buddy's lacking any balance
Always falling on his head,
An old tail docking injury
Left him with a stub instead.

It's hard to focus on our breath
When panting's all we hear
For those who need a Greenie
Front can smell just like the rear,

But at the end we're all relaxed
In Savasana we lay,
No need to rise in Mountain pose
In our peaceful place we'll stay.

Two Dogs

The moment my nose is alerting me
A bewitching I can't ignore,
A deliciousness wafts abundantly
Saliva pooling on the floor.

While you're busy with your ball obsession
I've lost all interest in to steal,
I'll be waiting by the kitchen counter
To eat gravity's grand reveal.

Going Out With the Dogs

I let the dogs out one more time
Their last call of the night,
I stepped out too, to view the stars
Full moon a lovely sight.

North wind is chilly in my gown
It's only for a bit,
I watch the dogs do circles
Decide I'm going to sit.

Surrounded by all woodland trees
No prying eyes to stare,
Except for critters of the night
Who really couldn't care.

Dogs finished with their dumps and squats
And sniffs to satisfy,
They head straight for the doggie door
In single file they fly.

Rising up to grab the doorknob
I find I've locked me out,
Standing keyless in my nightgown
No alternate reroute.

I'm thinking past the panic
No other way I know,
But getting down on hands and knees
Through doggie door I go.

Coming Home

My bark announces your arrival. I am tap dancing on the floor. Cat has magically levitated to the counter, with her dagger-throwing stare.

Door handle happily turning. I spin for effect. My paws greet your chest, a half hug. That crazy tail of mine, whacking the cabinet door, rattling all the dishes awake. Cat now appearing on recliner's highest perch, slits for eye, most disturbing daggers.

Work shoes discarded with a short trip to the bathroom. I cleaned the cat box today. Will you notice? You're good at noticing. You notice.

You reach for your play shoes, my favorite shoes. I gather the balls in my mouth, one, two, three balls. I grin showing you. I like your laughter. I try picking up more balls. Someday I will fit all ten. Then you will howl with laughter.

Back in the kitchen, Cat at the window now, gazing out, making her eerie clicking sounds, incantations on unsuspecting feeder visitors.

Maybe I'll see Squirrel, enticing me to a game of tag. But I need to keep my focus on my balls. You really love playing Throw, ball or Frisbee, your favorite game. I'm happy to bring it back to you, keeping Throw going. Sometimes I spice it up a bit, returning ball with leaves or tasty soil, and always generous with the slobber. It makes you smile.

Next is delightful dinner. In the kitchen Cat is pacing a path on the counter. Don't let that innocent mew confuse you. You're only needed for your can opening skills. She'd just as well eat you, and me too. I sleep with one eye open in your absence.

Now in relaxing room, will you notice the coffee table leg? It was in my way today as I chewed my Kong. You notice, much too loudly. Don't you remember yesterday? It was in the way of your socked foot. This is clearly better for both of us. How did the vase of flowers get on the floor? You really notice.

Cat mystically appears on the sofa, mocking me with her bewitching eyes. I am sure this is her wizardry.

Fledgling Season

When taking out the trash one day
I found a baby bird,
I didn't spy a nest nearby
No parents to observe.

"Well, where'd you come from little guy?"
I asked the fledgling dear,
I scooped him up to relocate
Set on an Elm branch near.

Minutes later I heard a peep
Outside my window screen,
The baby bird sat on the ground
His beak began to preen.

Went out again to lift him up
He tried to hop away,
Back on the branch for Mom to feed
Assured he wouldn't stay.

I guess each time he flutters down
He'll practice and perfect,
All I get for helping him, is
Mom squawking her object.

Cats are peering out the slider
I see him bouncing by,
Dear exploring, feathered fledgling

Please quickly learn to fly.

Keeping our domestic fur-babies separate from
wildlife protects them from predators and
keeps them from being predators.

My Cat

Big yawn and yoga stretch
Awake now from your nap,
You press yourself against my leg
Then jump upon my lap.

Your little motor's running
As I start to stroke your fur,
You eat the treats I give you
Between your mews and purr.

As I sit at my computer
Your body blocks my view,
A gentle walk across my keys
Adding texts from 'shift' to 'Q'.

What's crawling on the ceiling?
Your wide eyes fixed in stare,
Seeing ghosts again my cat?
There's really nothing there.

On my project there you lay
Tail twitching to some beat,
And daring my objections
Guess no work I will complete.

Are you in the mood for play?
You favorite toys I can bring,
It's fun to chase the red dot

Or feathers on the string.

You glide with grace across the room
Pounce on your prey with flair,
Chew on your mouse beside me
Your toe beans in the air.

Drinking from the kitchen sink
Many clever acts you do,
Pole dancing on your scratching post
All things that make you, 'You'.

You launch now from the ottoman
Find sun that's streaming in,
The perfect spot to preen yourself
It's time to nap again.

Little Spy

I hear a vibrating vibrato
An encroachment on my rest,
Your unwelcoming intrusion
No fly has ever been a guest.

My darting eyes are keeping time
As you circumvent the room,
While using wall like trampolines
I plot your impending doom.

I unsheathe my claws to swat you down
I will catch you in midair,
But you're suctioned to the ceiling now
With three thousand eyes you stare.

You disappear and disappoint
Only for a shortened bout,
My twitching ears can hear you buzz
Heightened senses seek you out.

You've gone behind the window blinds
Your grey shadow meets my eye,
I'm dismantling your hiding spot
Focused capture of the spy.

About the Author

As a youngster, Diane wrote stories from her imagination and illustrated them in crayon. She called them "books" and still has some of them today.

She went on the major in English in High School with the goal of becoming an author.

After attending a couple of years at Pikes Peak State College, she experienced motherhood and started two businesses.

One being a pet-sitting business, which she still enjoys doing.

She loves spending time with her three grandchildren, reading poetry and creating art. She has organized several fundraisers for non-profits and donates art to animal rescues.

www.ingramcontent.com/pod-product-compliance
Lightning Source LLC
Chambersburg PA
CBHW052036150726
48002CB00002B/640